Master of my time

my time

A practical guide to a simpler life

BEATRIZ GONZÁLEZ / MARÍA TERESA SHÖB

Master of my Time:
A Practical Guide to a Simpler Life
Copyright ©2018, Beatriz González / María Teresa Shöb
Original title: Mi tiempo soy yo
English translation © Alison Dent
© Cover and inside illustrations: Enrique Rodríguez Jiménez
Cover design: Graphic Design Department Podiprint

1st Edition 2018 - Podiprint
2nd Edition 2018 – Pukiyari Publishers

Internet: www.masteringmytime.com

ISBN-10: 1-63065-105-2
ISBN-13: 978-1-63065-105-3

Legal Deposit: MA 888-2018

PUKIYARI PUBLISHERS
www.pukiyari.com

(DEDICATION)

Contents

Introduction

Time is one of the most valuable resources we have and more often than not, we waste it.

In spite of us knowing that no moment can ever be recovered or made available to us again, we do not give time the importance it deserves.

Its inefficient use can leave us feeling stuck and frustrated because although we want to make better use of our time, we don't seem able to do so. This means that we are left exhausted by the effort required to deal with daily life and the things we have to do "come what may".

It is then, when our interest in managing time optimally is sparked, that we can attain the true time for our lives that we deserve.

When we talk about productivity, improvements and performance, an image comes to mind of companies whose main objective is to achieve efficient results by implementing strategies that make the best and maximum use of time and resources. However, we rarely think that something like this may be just as effective in an even more important enterprise, namely within our own homes.

Knowing the significant results achieved by the Japanese car manufacturer, Toyota, as a result of implementing a quality management method known as Kaizen (continuous improvement), we were curious to put it into practice in our homes and thus experience its usefulness first hand.

The "5 S" are five steps that belong to the Kaizen method. These techniques form the foundation of this guide, which we have applied to our home life.

We have gradually adapted these techniques and enhanced them with another equally useful and effective method known as KonMarie.

Marie Kondo, in her book, *The Life-Changing Magic of Tidying Up*, not only gives us guidelines for the practical side of tidying up, but also shows us how using them can lead to an improvement in happiness and mental well-being.

How many times do we hear people say, "I do not have time for..."?

If we were to draw up a list of everything we would like to be doing right now, we would see what things give us the greatest pleasure or comfort, and what really fills us with joy and happiness. Most of which we keep putting off because we say we do not have the time.

So why not make a choice to have more time to share activities with the people we love? Why not choose to have more time to do what we want or would like to do at any given moment without feeling stressed or needing to hurry?

We suggest that you start by making small changes to your environment and by doing so you will see how you can gain more time to do what you want to do, or just enjoy "doing nothing", without feeling guilty or overwhelmed by everything that "has to be done".

You can achieve it

The first suggestion is to put some of these strategies into practice in your immediate environment, namely your home. From here you will soon begin to feel the difference in living with an order and simplicity that will permeate your inner being and allow you to better manage your time. By living according to such order and simplicity, you will be a more decisive and practical person.

You can make it work

It is usually said that by changing yourself you can change your environment, but here we want to invite you to experience the opposite, "changing your environment can allow you to change".

Each step is designed to be carried out attentively, by tapping into your most creative side, so that each decision you make is accompanied by a feeling of pleasure and fulfilment.

This step will require perseverance and discipline; two habits that will help determine your final success.

Our main objective is to reclaim the time that flies away from us every day, the time that we do not get to enjoy, the time that we are unable to LIVE consciously.

As you learn to carry out this method, you will notice that the time invested is just the right and necessary amount for it to be effective. At the same time, you can enjoy it while you are doing it, a good enough reason to make every moment unique, special and different.

You can do it

How?

- By creating harmony among your possessions.
- By simplifying your daily routine of tasks, activities and objectives.
- By only choosing such things that are useful and durable.
- By ensuring that everything you possess is absolutely necessary and practical.
- By "self-reflecting" on how you feel when you live surrounded by order.

Change your environment

The main objective is to visualize a scheme or structure that will help you simplify your tasks.

At first, you will need to invest a certain amount of time in carrying out each step, but the interesting thing is that this laborious part happens just once. After that, you'll want to repeat the cycle, but it will now be easier and faster because there will be fewer things to deal with, and your idea of how you want your environment to look, will be clearer.

You might start with your bedroom and in particular with your wardrobe. You will find it easier to start with something you are most familiar with. For example, your clothes: deciding what you wear most often, what you feel most comfortable wearing or are most at ease in. The dynamic to follow would be to repeat this process with each garment.

The first thing you need to do is empty the entire contents of your closet, clean it thoroughly and if necessary repair any damage.

It is important that you gather together all the clothes you

have stored in other places of your house (such as other cup-
boards, boxes, storage rooms, dressing rooms, etc.) and place
them altogether in one place. Pile them up somewhere where they
will not get in the way of your daily chores and can be left until
you have finished the selection process and assigned them a new
'home'.

Practical implementation

Steps to follow:

1. Select and sort

2. Order and organize

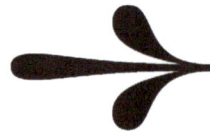

5. Develop habits and discipline

4. Standardize and label

3. Clean and maintain

Step 1
Select and Sort

The selection process

You should carry out the selection process quietly and consciously. It will probably take longer than initially expected. The effectiveness of the main objective, "to leverage your time effectively", depends on it.

Out of all your clothes, we are going to choose the ones we really want to keep by taking the garments one by one and asking ourselves, "Do I feel comfortable in this?", "Do I wear it often?". Or as Marie Kondo suggests, "Does it make me happy?".

Once you have selected what you want to keep, everything else can be donated, given away or even perhaps sold. You will probably be amazed to discover that you have lots of clothes that you never actually wear, taking up space in your wardrobe from one year to the next.

Get rid of everything you are not going to keep as soon as possible. This will clear some space and thus further facilitate the task, as well as avoid the temptation of retaining items and ending up as you were before.

At this point in the process, we suggest you reflect on your real needs, tastes and preferences, based on the following questions:

- Do I need everything I have kept?
- Do I enjoy having the closet packed full of things that I don't use?
- Am I aware of the time and space I will have to invest in managing all these things?
- Do I gratefully appreciate all that I have that makes me happy?

While selecting your clothes, it is a good idea to experience the change you are applying to your environment, feeling it from the 'outside-in', as well as from the 'inside-out', and paying special attention to what is happening within you.

Answering the following questions might help you to immerse yourself in the experience:

- How do I feel seeing what I have?
- Does it tell me something about myself, my tastes, my way of thinking, my way of being?
- How do I feel about keeping only what makes me feel good?
- What have I discovered about myself?

The sorting process

Now that you have selected the clothes you wish to keep, you can move on to the process of sorting them into categories: pants with pants, t-shirts with t-shirts, socks with socks, etc.

This step helps us realize whether we have what we need or if there are things that should be replaced because they are damaged or worn out.

After the sorting process is complete, you will choose an appropriate container to consolidate all garments of the same category together so they are not scattered about.

Once this step is completed, you can place them where you think they will be easily and quickly accessed, taking into account the things that are used most often. For example, placing them somewhere in the closet where they can be easily accessed, by being easily seen.

For example, if you practice a particular sport on a regular basis, it is easier to have all the clothes you need for that sport together so you do not waste time searching for every single item around the house.

Step 2
Order and Organize

Order cultivates personal well-being.

By putting our environment in order, we also put our lives in order. As we free up more space, selecting what we want to keep and looking for the best place to put it, we are also going through a process of selection within ourselves.

It's curious to see how easy it seems to organize a physical space, and yet we often find it difficult to put our inner space in order, when in fact the required procedure to follow is very similar.

Self-reflection allows us to experience our personal development on a daily basis.

You are discovering what you like, what you are fond of, the importance you give to comfort and well-being, and how you take care of yourself and pamper and love yourself.

When we live within an orderly environment, we feel its influence on our way of thinking, behavior and feelings. We are reminded of another perfect order that surrounds us and constantly invites us to live in its harmony.

In nature, everything flows, its balance turns the difficult into the easy, making us feel perfectly attuned to its flow and harmony.

We can consider this step by asking the following types of questions

- How do I feel now?
- Do I feel connected to nature?
- Do I feel connected to myself?
- Where do I place myself within my priorities?

Remember, when you pamper and love yourself, and you take special care in selecting whatever you buy and in doing what you want to do, you are helping to give meaning to your life.

Take a moment and feel:

- Do I really care about myself?
- Have I already changed from feeling overwhelmed and stressed by everything I have to do, to feeling satisfied when I see that I am surrounded only by things that I have chosen in total freedom and full consciousness?

How to fold and where to place?

Once you have a place reserved for each garment, fold it and place it where it should now belong.

This step is about practice until each garment is where and how you would like it to be.

The folding method suggested by Marie Kondo is ideal for such practicality. Clothes can be placed vertically like books on a shelf, thus allowing for quick access without disturbing the other clothes around them. She suggests placing these folded clothes in drawers or boxes.

After some trial and error, you will finally arrive at the folding method and container which best suits your needs. And while you fold and place your clothes like this, you will see that everything stays in order for much longer.

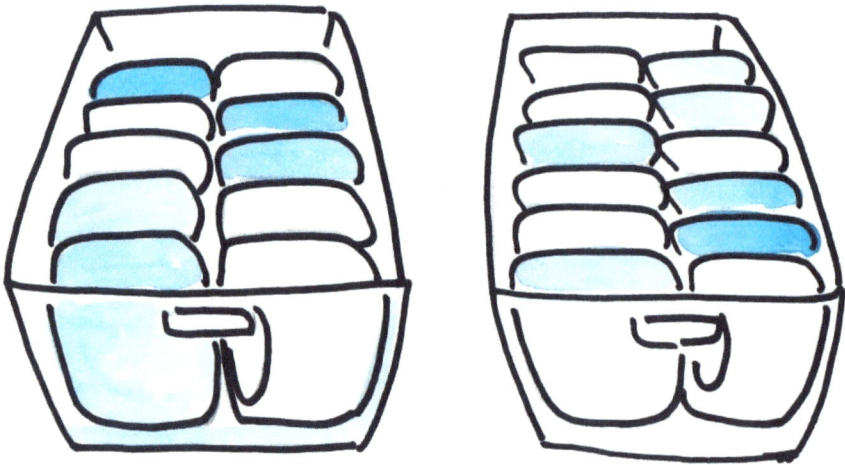

Step 3
Clean and Maintain

It is important to determine what makes things dirty and either eliminate the source of this dirt or find a solution to reduce or eliminate the cause. We should bear this point in mind while we apply this process to the different rooms of the house most exposed to dirt due to their constant use, such as the bathroom, the kitchen, the living room, etc.

To do this, instead of waiting for something to get dirty, we should try to keep it clean with a daily routine of just a few minutes. This will constitute a natural rhythm and form part of your daily activities, so that you only have to spend a few moments doing this, rather than hours it might otherwise take to do a thorough cleaning periodically.

For example, whenever you go to the bathroom and wash your hands and the mirror gets splashed, have a cloth nearby to wipe up afterwards, or even better keep a nice scented cleaner on hand, spray the mirror and then wipe it. This gives the bathroom a nice ambiance.

It is very useful to place wipes, a mop and cloths near the places that accumulate dirt quickly so that they can be used regularly and thus help maintain cleanliness. Also, to keep things in order, have some containers or boxes on hand that could be used as temporary storage for the things found out of place. This allows you to clear them away and put them back in their proper place when you have more time.

We invite you to take a few minutes to think and determine where the hotbeds of dirt are in your house, where you have to spend the most time cleaning and which areas most frequently. How do you think you can resolve this issue?

Step 4
Standardize and Label

Visual aids are most effective

A very effective way to gain time is to delegate or break-down tasks, turning something that seems difficult into something easy.

How?

By using signs, photos, drawings, illustrations, posters, labels and so on, we can identify things more quickly.

In this way, when someone needs to take out an object or put it back after using it, they can do so without having to ask someone else, who might not be able to tell them at that precise moment, where it belongs.

It is worth remembering what we previously suggested in Step 2, that everything belonging to the same category should go in the same place. For example: keys with keys, pens with pens, scissors with scissors, etc. This will save us a lot of time by not having to go scurrying around the house looking for something when it is needed.

Step 5
Develop Habits and
Discipline

Continuous improvement

To be consistent in your daily life is one of the most important rules that must be followed for each step to work optimally. Perseverance will turn routine into habit, establishing itself as something we do naturally every day.

As you make progress in achieving your goals, you will develop a skill that will bring you closer to that which really pleases you and to how and when you want to do things. It is then that you will arrive at a moment of transformation, a moment of feeling different. If it has not already happened during the process, now might be a good time to take note of how you feel when you live within order and harmony.

A very useful way of being able to accomplish this is to have a notebook or journal where you can plan the activities to be done, giving priority to the most important things you have to do.

Applying these five steps to every room in the house will allow order and harmony to reign in your home, and therefore your life.

Now is the time to own less but enjoy more; that's the next step.

From Doing to Being

How?

Enjoying and feeling each moment as unique

Enjoying my time, enjoying my space, from the peace within; sharing moments with my friends, with my family, without urgency; slowly sipping my favorite drink, savoring its aroma, tasting it while silence fills the intimacy that my heart is longing for, allowing perfect warmth and comfort to emanate from deep within me to be pleasantly acknowledged and fill me with a perfect sense of well-being.

THIS STEP IS AN INVITATION TO FEEL....

Through my senses, I´m going to design my world as I want it to be and then I will start to walk boldly, confidently and gratefully in a welcoming environment.

What would you like to do or enjoy right now? What is stopping you?

Share

Accompany others

When we experience the deep peace that is the result of the path travelled through our life, we feel the need to share it with others.

Recognizing ourselves in others leads us to connect with our true essence. Every moment is unique; this is our time and giving our best of ourselves to others is the greatest legacy we can leave.

When you are in a state of true listening, of patience and acceptance, without judgement, you are transmitting a feeling of welcome that inspires others to want to feel the same.

Perhaps ask yourself the following:

- Do I feel the need to share?
- Do I see myself offering something to others?
- How is my listening?
- How is my breathing? Am I aware of how I breathe?

- **Do I breathe tranquility? Do I breathe peace?**

Every step that we have suggested above can be equally transforming if you apply it not only to your environment but also to your life.

Stop for a moment, take a long deep breath and allow yourself to feel. Observe your thoughts without any judgement and give yourself permission to express everything you feel as it arises. Ask yourself if your time is truly yours; if you are making optimal use of it; if you live it as if it is the most precious thing you have; if you invest in what you really like and crave. In short, ask yourself,
"Am I the master of my time?"

Beatriz González González

Beatriz has devoted a large part of her life to studying music. She holds a degree in Oboe and became a key member of the Havana National Symphony Orchestra. She carried on her postgraduate studies at the Royal Conservatory of Music in Madrid. She continued her professional training at Cadiz University, becoming an Expert in Music Therapy. Beatriz currently lives in Marbella where she was teaching at the Municipal Conservatory of Music.

She is a Mindfulness consultant and an Expert in Conscious Nutrition, having trained at the Transpersonal Development School in Madrid.

Beatriz currently works as a music teacher, Mindfulness consultant and facilitator in workshops on time management and organization in the home. These activities fit very well with her various roles as a woman who fully enjoys what she considers to be her great passions: her time, her family and her contribution to life.

María Teresa Schöb Wolniewitz

Maria Teresa worked for many years as an Airline Marketing consultant. She is a language teacher, facilitator of workshops on Philosophical Painting as a path to self-knowledge, and a facilitator of personal development and motivation workshops in both the private and the public sector.

She is a Biodynamic Craniosacral Therapist, the training for which led her to understand and experience selfless listening, which forms the basis of her work as a Mindfulness consultant.

From a young age, Maria Teresa was interested in and studied topics relating to personal development and motivation.

In recent years, she has been dedicated to the study and application of habits in order to be able to live with more aware- ness and learn to manage her time as effectively as possible while fully enjoying her life.

www.ingramcontent.com/pod-product-compliance
Lightning Source LLC
LaVergne TN
LVHW072111070426
835509LV00003B/117